The Life and Work of

Henry
Moore

Sean Connolly

Heinemann Library
Chicago, Illinois

Customer Service 888-454-2279
Visit our website at www.heinemannraintree.com

Designed by Jo Malivoire and Q2A Creative
Printed in China by South China Printing Company

10 09 08 07 06
10 9 8 7 6 5 4 3 2 1

New edition ISBN: 1-40348-491-0 (hardcover)
                    1-40348-502-X (paperback)

The Library of Congress has cataloged the first edition as follows:
Connolly, Sean, 1956-
                Henry Moore / Sean Connolly.
                        p. cm. — (The life and work of–) (Heinemann profiles)
                Includes bibliographical references and index.
                Summary: Introduces the life and work of Henry Moore, discussing his early years, life in England, and
        development as an artist.
                ISBN 1-57572-953-9
                1. Moore, Henry, 1898- Juvenile literature. 2. Sculptors-
        -England-Biography-Juvenile literature. [1. Moore, Henry, 1898-
        2. Sculptors 3. Art appreciation.] I. Title. II. Series.
        III. Series: Heinemann profiles.
        NB497.M6C65   1999
        730'. 92—dc21   99-14558
        [B]   CIP

Acknowledgments
The author and publishers are grateful to the following for permission to reproduce copyright material:
p. 4, *Portrait Studio, 1960*. p. 5, Henry Moore *Three Forms: Vertebrae*. p. 6, Henry Moore aged 11. p. 7, Castleford Grammar School's Roll of Honour. p. 8, Henry Moore convalescing at Castleford Grammar School, 1918. p. 9, Henry Moore *Small Animal Head 1921*. p. 10, Corner of Studio Adie Road 1928. p. 11, Henry Moore *Reclining Figure 1929*. p. 12, Henry Moore with West Wind 1928. p. 13, North wall of Headquarters of London Underground. p. 14, Corner of studio at 11a Parkhill Road Hampstead 1936. p. 15, Henry Moore *Reclining Figure 1936*. p. 17, Henry Moore *Two forms 1934*. p. 18, Lee Miller, Henry Moore in Holborn Underground, London 1943. p. 19, Henry Moore *Pink and Green Sleepers 1941*. p. 20, Lee Miller Archives, Henry Moore with Severini in Venice for the Biennale 1948. p. 21, Henry Moore *Madonna and child*. p. 22, Henry Moore carving *UNESCO Reclining Figure 1957-58*. p. 23 Henry Moore *Draped Reclining Figure 1952-53*. p. 24, Henry Moore in Top Studio 1954. p. 25, Henry Moore *Double Oval*. p. 26, Henry Moore working in new maquette studio 1978. p. 27, Henry Moore *Sheep Piece 1962-63*. p. 28, The Independent. p. 29, Henry Moore *Large Figure in a shelter 1952-53*. p. 16, Robert Harding Picture Library.

Cover photograph: *Family Group, 1944* - artist collection - Moore, Henry Spencer, reproduced by permission of Phillips the international fine art auctioneers UK, c. Bonhams, London, UK / Bridgeman Art Library.

The publishers would like to thank Nancy Harris for her assistance in the preparation of this book.

Some words in this book are in bold, **like this.** You can find out what they mean by looking in the Glossary.

Contents

Who was Henry Moore?

Henry Moore was a very important artist.
He made huge **sculptures** out of stone,
wood, and a metal called **bronze**. He also
made many drawings.

People from around the world asked Henry to make sculptures for them. This sculpture is in Dallas, Texas. Henry made it in 1978.

Early Years

Henry Moore was born on July 30 1898 in Castleford, England. His father was a **miner**. When Henry was 12 years old he went to Castleford Grammar School.

Henry was already good at art. When he was 16 years old his teachers asked him to **carve** this **roll of honor** for the school.

London and Paris

Henry fought in **World War I** for two years. In 1921 he began studying at the Royal College of Art in London. Two years later he visited Paris in France.

Henry saw many types of art in London and Paris. Henry made this **sculpture** of a small animal head in London in 1921.

Teaching

In 1925 Henry became a teacher at the Royal College of Art in London. He was also busy making his own **sculptures**. In 1928 he had an **exhibition** in London.

Henry **carved** his sculptures out of stone.
He liked to show people lying on their sides.
He made many sculptures like this one.

The Public Eye

Henry became more famous. When he was 31 he had his first **commission**. It was a huge **sculpture** for the London Underground subway.

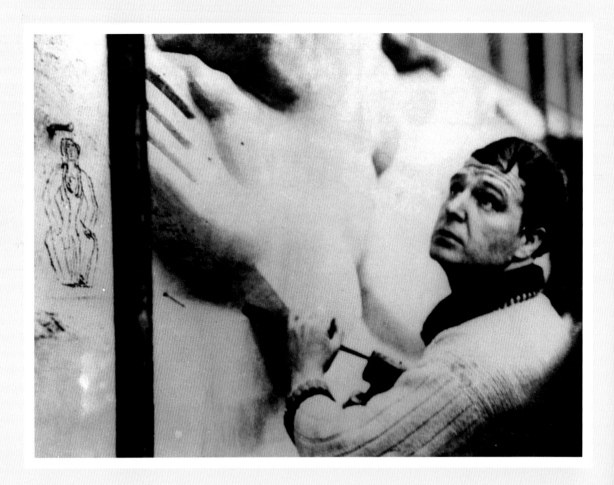

The title of this sculpture was *The North Wind*. It shows Henry's interest in stone, fire, water, and wind.

The Modern World

In the 1930s Henry became interested in **abstract art**. His **sculptures** began to look less like human beings and more like simple, rounded shapes.

Henry collected pebbles, stones, and shells to see how nature creates shapes. This statue shows Henry's interest in smooth, curved surfaces.

Getting Known

More and more people saw the beauty in Henry's large **sculptures**. They were **exhibited** in Europe and the United States. This is a picture of the Museum of Modern Art in New York City.

Henry sold this sculpture to the Museum of
Modern Art in New York City. It shows how
his sculptures were only partly **abstract**.
Here you can still see human shapes.

War Artist

World War II began in 1939. Two years later Henry became an official war artist. He drew the daily life of people living in London during the war.

These drawings are some of Henry's most powerful works. This one shows people trying to sleep while bombs explode outside.

Traveling the World

After the war Henry traveled around the world. He got many awards and prizes for his **sculptures**. This picture shows Henry and a friend in Venice, Italy.

Henry's prizes did not change his work. He made this **tender** sculpture of Mary and Jesus for a church in England.

Time for a Change

In the 1950s Henry tried new ways of working. Until then he **carved** directly from stone. Now he made many **sculptures** from **bronze** and wood.

Henry could make even bigger, smoother sculptures out of bronze. This sculpture of a woman is in London, England.

New Ideas

Henry also looked for new ideas. In the 1960s he began putting one shape inside another one. Many of these combined shapes created **hollow sculptures**.

Henry wanted people to look at his large sculptures from all sides. These two oval shapes seem alike at first. They only look different when you walk around them.

The Sculptor's Studio

Henry moved to Perry Green, north of London when London was bombed during the war. He was very happy there.

There were sheep in the field outside Henry's **studio**. In the 1970s Henry made many **sketches** of the sheep. He made this **sculpture** to go in the field.

An Active Life Ends

Mourning Henry Moore yesterday: Jeremy Thorpe; Lord Snowdon and Sir Hugh Casson; Moore's daughter Mary Danowski and her children; Michael Foot and his wife, Jill Craigie.

Friends pay tribute to Moore

FELLOW ARTISTS and friends of the sculptor Henry Moore paid their last respects at a memorial service in Westminster Abbey yesterday. Many of his surviving contemporaries including his widow, Irina, whom he married in 1929, were too frail to attend.

Sir Stephen Spender, the poet, told the congregation that Moore, who died in August, aged 88, was the seventh son of a Yorkshire miner who never considered anyone either socially superior or inferior to himself.

Sir Stephen, one of the last surviving members of Moore's avant-garde Hampstead artistic circle in the Thirties, delivered the address in a brisk, husky whisper. He remembered Moore's studio as a focal point for artists, including Ben Nicholson, the painter, and Barbara Hepworth, the sculptress.

He said that despite Moore's admiration for the abstract artists around him, "he told me he could never make an artefact which referred to nothing but itself".

Moore had confided to him: "Try as I might, my work always ended up looking like something, probably a reclining figure."

Sir Stephen quoted Sir Herbert Read, the poet and art critic, and a champion of Moore in the Thirties, saying that in his opinion the sculptor would have been the best possible ambassador from this planet to another.

Sir Stephen said: "He was an artist of great ingenuity and a man of great humanity." Moore had never forgotten the simplicity of his upbringing.

Dame Peggy Ashcroft, the actress, read the first lesson, not from the Bible but from the Apocrypha, the second book of Esdras. It concluded: "He who made all things, and searcheth out hidden things in hidden places, surely he knoweth your imagination, and what ye think in your hearts." The text was suggested to the Moore family by Westminster Abbey, because its words were so appropriate.

The second lesson, read by the Duke of Gloucester, was from Revelations, in the King James version, chosen because it is the one familiar to Moore's generation.

The congregation included the Prime Minister; Michael Foot, the former Labour leader; Sir Hugh Casson, the architect and painter; Sir Roy Strong, director of the Victoria and Albert Museum; Jeremy Thorpe, the former Liberal leader; John Profumo, the former Conservative Cabinet minister, Lord Snowdon and Sam Wanamaker, the film maker.

List of mourners, page 13

Henry still worked when he was more than 80 years old. He died on August 31 1986. He was 88 years old. There was a special service in Westminster Abbey in London when he died.

This **sculpture** is the largest **bronze** work that Henry ever made. Henry made it just one year before he died.

Timeline

1898	Henry Moore is born in Castleford, Yorkshire on July 30.
1910	Henry enters Castleford Grammar School.
1914–18	**World War I** is fought.
1917	Henry joins the Army and fights in World War I.
1921	Henry enters the Royal College of Art, London on a scholarship.
1924	Henry's first **sculptures** are shown in London.
1928	Henry's first one-man **exhibition** in London.
1929	Henry marries Irina Radestsky and completes major work for the London Underground.
1938	Henry takes part in the International Exhibition of **Abstract Art** in the Netherlands.
1939–45	**World War II** is fought.
1941	Henry is made an Official War Artist.
1940s	Henry has exhibitions in the United States, Australia, Belgium, and other countries.
1948	Henry wins International Prize for Sculpture in Venice.
1986	Henry dies in Perry Green, England on August 31.

Glossary

abstract art art that tries to show ideas rather than the way things look

bronze type of metal

carve cut into a shape

commission being asked to make a piece of art

exhibition public showing of art

hollow having an empty inside

miner someone who works underground to digging coal

roll of honor list of names of people who have fought in a war

sculpture piece of art that has been made out of stone, wood, or other materials

sketch another word for a drawing

studio place where an artist works

tender showing kindness and gentleness

World War I the war in Europe that lasted from 1914 to 1918

World War II the war that was fought in Europe, Africa, and Asia from 1939 to 1945

More Books to Read

Wolfe, Gillian. *Oxford First Book of Art.* New York: OUP, 2004.

More Sculptures to See

Two-Piece Reclining Figure, 1961. Henry Moore, Los Angeles County Museum of Art, Cal.

Large Arch, 1971. Henry Moore, Library Plaza, Columbus, Indiana.

The Dallas Piece, 1978. Henry Moore, City Hall Plaza, Dallas, Texas.

Index